THE PRICE
OF FRESH
Anointing

CHRIS G. ABAGA

THE PRICE OF FRESH *Anointing*

Rekindle Your First Love Remain On The Cutting Edge

Glit iTec & Trade

Published on Selar.co, Lulu, Rkobo, Rightway and Republished on Amazon by Glit iTec & Trade
PSQ129 U/Maigero Road, Kaduna Nigeria / 800244
09026557129 | glitpublishers@gmail.com

Glit iTec & Trade is committed to credibility and professionality in the publishing industry.

Book design copyright © 2016 by Tate Publishing, LLC. All rights reserved.
Cover design by Dante Rey Redido
Interior design by Mary Jean Archival

First Published in the United States of America 2016

ISBN: 978-1-68301-519-2
1. Religion / Christian Life / General
2. Religion / Christian Life / Devotional

Contents

Preface

ONE OF THE ministers of the gospel in my country (Nigeria) whom I have respect for and I regard as a mentor and spiritual leader is Pastor Enoch A. Adeboye, General Overseer of the Redeemed Christian Church of God (RCCG). Pastor Adeboye is paying the price to keep the fire of revival burning in his life and ministry. As a result of his enormous personal sacrifice for the gospel and continuous fervent intercessory prayer, the Holy Spirit has raised him up as a champion for Jesus! Through his lifestyle of humility, brokenness, and visionary leadership, the Redeemed Christian Church of God is spreading like wildfire to Africa, America, Europe, and other parts of the world. Pastor Adeboye receives a fresh word from God. He preaches and ministers with fresh power and amazing healings; diverse miracles are taking place during his meetings, which attract millions of people.

Concerning the enormity of price that Pastor E. A. Adeboye is paying to take the gospel to the nations of the world, Rebecca Bible-David shares something about the secret strength of Pastor Adeboye in her biography, *Enoch Adeboye: Father of Nations*:

> "Enoch Adeboye is a man of prayer and fasting. His children say they can count on their fingers, days when he is not fasting. Before many major crusades which attract millions of souls, Adeboye sometimes denies himself of food, for lengthy days. His kids sometimes get scared with the way he fasts for long days. And because of his tall sleep becomes uncontrollable, he doesn't retire to bed, instead, he gathers hard stones on the floor and kneel on it. By doing this, the stones are painful and uncomfortable so this would definitely keep him awake to pray all night. At other times, when he does not kneel on stones, he would start climbing stairs up and down in prayer".

In Leviticus chapter six that talks about the law of the burnt offering, the Bible makes it clear that the priest must ensure the fire shall be kept burning on the altar of the temple day and night:

> Then the Lord said the Moses, "Give Aaron and his sons the following instructions regarding the whole burnt offering. The burnt offering must be left on the altar until the next morning, and the altar fire

must be kept burning all night. The next morning, after dressing in his special linen clothing and undergarments, the priest on duty must clean out the ashes of the burnt offering and put them besides the altar. Then he must change back into his normal clothing and carry the ashes outside the camp to a place that is ceremonially clean. Meanwhile, the fire on the altar must be kept burning; it must never go out. Each morning the priest will add fresh wood to the fire and arrange the daily whole burnt offering on it. He must then burn the fat of the peace offerings on top of this daily whole burnt offering. Remember the fire must be kept burning on the altar at all times. It must never go out. (Lev. 6:8–13)

Some preachers and ministers of the gospel go to fake sources to get power (anointing), whereas the secret power for service lies on their fingertips. Unlike the fire on the altar in the temple—which must be kept burning on the altar continuously—for some Christians, the fire of revival on the altar of their hearts has died down. They no longer sense the tingling sensation of the burning touch of God's love in their lives. Some Christians are living in defeat. They have lost the joy of the Lord, and they are wondering: What is the price of fresh anointing? What is the secret of sustaining the anointing and keeping the fire of revival and the freshness of the presence of the Holy Spirit burning brightly upon our hearts till Jesus comes? How can someone, who has fallen into sin and the trap of the enemy with guilt and shame trailing him, experience full restoration and start enjoying the favour of the Lord once again? Is it possible to rekindle our first love and remain the cutting?

This book, *The Price of Fresh Anointing*, has come at the right season to offer you a few tips, which will assist you to reignite the revival flame afresh and guide you to remain on the cutting edge of Christian service and intimate walk with the Lord. Receiving a fresh word from the Lord is not cheap. There is a price to be paid; that is, if we are willing to pay whatever price is required to become all that God wants us to be.

May the Holy Spirit help you overcome every obstacle and start your journey to becoming a world class champion!

Chris Abaga
Abuja, Nigeria

God Uses Broken Vessels

For thE Anointing of the Holy Spirit to come strong and stay fresh in a person's life, he or she must be willing to pay a great price. God does not just randomly pick any person on the streets of any city in the world or in some remote village and automatically bestow on him the double anointing of His divine presence. The process of divine preparation in God's hands takes time. Fresh anointing comes with the tortuous process of divine preparation in the tough wilderness experiences in life. There are no exceptions to this rule. Show me a man or woman who is anointed and consecrated with the oil of anointing of the Holy Spirit and I will show you a person who is secretly carrying a heavy cross on his shoulders and walking in brokenness and surrender.

Many people desire to be mightily used by God to change the world and leave behind a lasting legacy for generations to come, but they are not willing to pay the price. They are not ready to submit to divine dealings in the school of brokenness. They fail to understand that God uses broken vessels. There are no short cuts to greatness and fresh anointing. If the good hand of God is upon your life to use you in fresh revival fires, your road to greatness at the top will be extremely rough, laden with pain, sorrow, sickness, poverty, disappointment, and betrayal. The degree of your potential greatness, promotion, and destiny will likely determine the depth of suffering you may be forced to confront in life.

Unless you are able to come to that point in your life where people consider you a complete liability with shame and controversy trailing you and starring at you on the face, you may not be ready yet to be a vessel of honor in the hands of our Lord, Jesus Christ. Always remember that fresh anointing is costly. God will not use you for special purpose to cause maximum impact until He Himself is convinced beyond doubt that you are dead, buried, and forgotten by people. In fact, when "God looks for a man to groom him, prepare him and set him in a place for a special assignment, He will begin to work in areas of his life usually not thought of by others. God must test him in every area, not only physically, but also emotionally, mentally, and financially, until" his life has been tempered by that suffering. When he endures in this place, then he is chosen to be a special envoy and God will back him with all of heaven's resources.".

Understanding Brokenness

> Brokenness is the work of God by which He strips us of self-sufficiency so that the character of Christ may shine through us. True brokenness is when God strips us of self-sufficiency to the extent that we have no strength left to fix ourselves. When God blocks every exist, we have tried to take by our own ability and we finally come to see that He alone is our answer, we make a life changing discovery. Remember that God's power is reserved for those who have given up trying to do it in their own strength or to accomplish if for their own ends.

Being broken is the process in which we are willing to to pay the price for fresh anointing. However, being broken does not necessarily mean experiencing tragedy because "many people suffer tragedy without drawing closer to God or even acknowledging Him. So, the issue in brokenness is not so much our circumstances but our response."

The truth is, a kernel of wheat must be planted in the soil. Unless it dies, it will be alone as a single seed. But if it dies, it will produce many new kernels and a plentiful harvest of new lives. Those who love their life in this world will lose it. Those who despise their life in this world will keep it for eternal life. According to Jesus, the seed must die; if it doesn't, it is completely useless and cannot serve any meaningful purpose in God's kingdom. The seed must die because life flows out of broken things. Remember that seeds cannot grow in hard soil. The soil must be broken up, the seed planted and allowed to stay in the soil until it is rotten and broken. After which, new life emerges beautifully out of the soil.

Notice that Jesus was not just teaching an idealistic principle. By His death on a cross and resurrection, Jesus demonstrated practically the principle of dying to live. Against all odds, Jesus was willing to submit to the divine will and have His body mutilated and broken on the cross. He paid on awesome price for sin. The Sinless One died in the hands of sinners and was buried. His body decomposed and decayed. But on the third day, Jesus rose triumphantly from the dead and from the grave, with newness of life to offer salvation to the world (Heb. 12:2). In the same manner, you cannot grow with limitless capacity and potential unless God allows you to go through tough times. The Lord will clip your wings and you will not be able to rely from people, money, fame, and family ties, which you tend to make as the object of your trust. They may be completely removed so that God has room and liberty to work in your life. God will put you in a tight corner, and bring you to a dead-end street where you cry and shout for help. Unfortunately in the wilderness, there is no help nearby. What you discover in there may shock you to silence and solitude, and perhaps, the sound of water falls, sweet music of birds (all for free) and the threatening sound from wild animals.

Broken vessels depend less and less on people and their opinion about them. Brokenness removes human dependence, which we cherish dearly and tends to limit our ability to perform at maximum capacity. Lack of brokenness inhibits our ability to soar to great heights. We all know how limiting human dependence is; whatever help people may give you—apart from divine assistance—will take you nowhere. However, when we reach a point in our walk with God when we depend less on people and learn to place our total trust in the sovereign God, then God takes our weakness and exchanges it for His strength, empowering us with supernatural ability to soar to great heights.

> Don't put your confidence in powerful people; there is no help from you there. When their breathing stops, they return to the earth, and in a moment all their plans come to an end. But happy are those who have the God of Israel as their helper, whose hope is in the Lord their God. He is the one who made heaven and earth, the sea, and everything in them. He is the one who keeps every promise forever, who gives justice to the oppressed and food to the hungry. (Ps. 146:3–7)

To be able to possess a better understanding of the subject of brokenness, we need to answer some important questions related to this subject. Why does God break His servants? What are the benefits of brokenness? What instruments does God use to melt or mould His chosen vessels? What are the symptoms of an unbroken vessel?

Why Brokenness?

Some people wonder that if I am in the center of God's will, why would I suffer? Why does God take His people through the difficult thorny path of sorrow, heartache, tragedy, disappointment, terrible shame, and agony before establishing His purpose and anointing them for ministry? Why shouldn't those who are serving the Lord faithfully be shielded from problems? What is the benefit of serving God if all I receive at the end of the day is sorrow, shame, and disgrace? Why does God take pains in breaking His servants as a price for fresh anointing? What does God really have in mind?

First of all, it is absolutely important for us to understand that in God's economy and His scheme of things, life flows out of broken things. Consequently, God breaks everything He uses because unless the jar is broken, the oil cannot flow. In the symbolic anointing and preparation of the body of Jesus for burial by Mary (Mark 4:3–9), it is abundantly clear that without the breaking process—without breaking her alabaster (jar) of costly perfume—the oil in the jar would not have been poured out to anoint Jesus. When the jar is broken, the oil can flow. Similarly, unless we are willing to be broken, willing to have our public reputation shattered and battered, we cannot be a vessel of honor in the hands of the Almighty God. Brokenness precedes fresh fire and fresh oil of divine presence.

Secondly, God breaks His servants in order to fit them into His perfect plan. Let us not forget that the airplanes we fly in and the cars we drive are all made out of hard steel iron rods. But before the various diverse shapes of the different spare parts are constructed, the manufacturers are wise enough to process the iron rods through intense heat to be melted and molded into the different specified shapes because it is heated fire that is capable of bending a steel iron rod. And once the metal rod goes through the right degree of heat, it automatically melts and can now be bent into specified shape. So it is with our lives; it is the correct degree of heat of troubled times applied to our lives and circumstances that is capable of melting and molding us. We go through God's chosen processing plant of trials and tribulations in order to be molded and remolded to fit into God's eternal plan and purpose for our lives. It is the Holy Spirit who carefully supervises the melting, molding, and remoulding process to make sure that we have been formed into the right shape for the right purpose at the right time. The Holy Spirit ensures that in the passage of time, we are able to discover God's definite purpose and destiny. It is the Holy Spirit who fits us where we belong in God's agenda and plan. Nobody knows what he or she will become in life at the beginning, except the

Holy Spirit. So really, brokenness precedes the discovery and fulfilment of destiny. There is no greater joy than when you know God's plan, purpose. and destiny in your life. God places heaven's resources at your disposal for you to accomplish His perfect will.

Thirdly, brokenness is necessary because God cannot share His glory with any person (Is. 42:8). God cannot pour His anointing on flesh. God cannot trust those who are full of themselves and egotistical of their own accomplishments and achievements in His presence. The anointing cannot fall on flesh, lest we dare to stretch our filthy hands to touch God's glory. Brokenness precedes spiritual power.

Moses was not yet ready for spiritual power and double anointing until his own flesh had been tested in the wilderness of Midian, where he was a wanderer and a fugitive for forty long years. After forty years of rugged, lonely, and hard wilderness experience, Moses was mightily anointed (Exod. 3:1–3) for public ministry when he submitted to God's painful dealings without complaining and grumbling. The Lord made sure that Moses was brought to the place of complete submission and obedience. Moses' pride, reputation, and dreams were totally crushed before he qualified for the anointing.

In the case of King David, even though the anointing fell on him quite early in his life (at the tender age of seventeen), he was not yet ready for ministry until his life had been tempered by thirteen years of struggle. King David was being pursued by his master, King Saul, who sought to kill David because of Saul's insecurities and wicked suspicion that David might take over the kingdom from him. King David was anointed (1 Sam. 16); but his anointing needed to be *cooked* and *heated* in the hot furnace of pain and *tough times* before the *fresh oil* of the presence of the Holy Spirit can flow through him in order to touch the lives of his people. You may be highly gifted and anointed but unless you submit your gift and calling in God's hands in the school of brokenness, fresh oil cannot flow. You cannot receive fresh word from the throne of God without brokenness. Because King David paid the price, God anointed him for a special service. It is in the book of Psalm that we set to know something about King David's anointing (Psalm 89:20).

The great Apostle Paul in the New Testament was mightily anointed by God to the extent that even handkerchiefs or aprons having contact with his body had supernatural power to heal the sick and deliver people from demonic possession (Act 19:11–12). Paul enjoyed a high degree of anointing from the Holy Spirit in his ministry. However, in order to ensure that he was constantly positioned to bring glory to God, he was given a chronic and debilitating problem, which kept him humble, reminding him of the grace of God throughout the growing years of his ministry.

> Even though I have received wonderful revelations from God. But to keep me from getting puffed up, I

was given a thorn in my flesh, a messenger from Satan to torment me and keep me from getting proud. Three different times I begged the Lord to take it away. Each time he said, "My gracious favour is all you need. My power works best in your weakness." So now I am glad to boast about my weaknesses, so that the power of Christ may work through me. Since I know it is all for Christ good. I am quite content with my weaknesses and with insults, hardships persecutions, and calamities. For when I am weak, then I am strong. (2 Cor. 12:7–10)

So we can understand that the primary prerequisite for the anointing and for fresh oil for global ministry is not necessarily theological training or overseas connections or financial weight or megachurch, but a broken and yielded life in the Master's hands. Self-centeredness is one of the greatest obstacles to fresh revival fire. God desires to carry out special work in our lives so that in the process of serving Him, we might learn a vital and eternal lesson: Never ever touch God's glory! Remember the words of John the Baptist, "He [Jesus] must become greater and greater, and I must become less and less" (John 3:30).

If you dare to pay the price and become a diligent student in the school of brokenness, you will be given a measure of divine presence and authority so that you may have an impact on your generation and future generations for Jesus. Always bear in mind that fresh quality anointing comes from God through tough training and divine preparation.

Benefits of Brokenness

Someone may ask, what do we stand to gain by the pruning and breaking process? Even though God has a definite purpose and plan in passing His servants through the refining fire of tough times, what are really the benefits to us personally when we become diligent students in the school of brokenness? There are several benefits of the broken life; let us examine a few of the benefits.

1. Brokenness helps us to enjoy God's unqualified peace and favor. The pain helps us to conquer worry, anxiety, and fear, which are big *killer diseases* today and tend to threaten the peaceful existence of many people globally. Worry leads to diseases such as hypertension, ulcer, and depression. If these ailments and human conditions are left unchecked, it can bring death. Broken people are so clam, collected, and cool that nothing seems to bother them. Their calm spirit has been acquired during the cocooning stage of dormancy when God clips their wings and they are forced to die to the spirit of anxiety and impatience. Broken people enjoy perfect peace (Is. 26:3), which passes all understanding (Phil. 4:6–7).

2. When we are broken, God becomes our total source, our El-Shaddai, the one who is more than enough. Because of God's painful dealings in your life, you are brought to the place of less and less dependence on people and more and more complete trust in God's ability to meet your needs. King David's faith developed and matured during those thirteen years of rugged wilderness training in the school of brokenness. As a result, David grew up to know God as his only provider. In 1 Chronicles 29:11–2, he declares:

> Yours, O Lord is the greatness, the power, the glory, the victory, and the majesty. Everything in the heaven and on earth is yours, O Lord, and this is your kingdom. We adore you as the one who is over all things. Riches and honour come from you alone, for you rule over everything. Power and might are in your hands, and it is at your discretion that people are made great and given strength.

When you know God as your source and you come to a place where God takes over in your life, no matter what happens, you can never be stranded. Perhaps, you are facing a tough embarrassing financial challenge at this moment. However, because you are God's precious child, the apple of His eyes (Zech. 2:8), and His treasured possession, take my word for it that no matter what happens, you will never be stranded. Supernatural provision—many times from strange sources not deemed possible—has been the cherished experience of believers through the centuries. Many pioneer missionaries working in remote fields have great stories to tell of how God came through for them and made provision at the very critical hour of need.

Sadhu Sundar Singh (1889–1929) was an Indian missionary evangelist, who was called by God at the tender age of fourteen, began his missionary journeys to Northern India and the forbidden territories of Tibet at the age of sixteen. Throughout his missionary journeys to these dangerous places, Sadbu walked barefoot (without sandals on his feet) and carrying no food and money (in order to emulate the self sacrificial lifestyle of Jesus Christ as much as possible). Sadhu Singh trekked through thousands of miles across the Himalayan Mountains in the bitter cold without warm covers or shelter. Yet, it was in the midst of these risky journeys that God showed up to provide for his needs time after time. God sent people to rescue him from near-death encounters with ruthless llamas in Tibet who were bent on stopping anyone from entering Tibet with the gospel message.

God makes a way where there is no way, and it is in the wilderness experience of tough times that you are able to truly prove the reality of God's love in your life.

> I look up to the mountains does my help come from there? My help comes from the Lord who made the heavens and earth? He will not let you stumble and fall; the one who watches over you will not sleep. Indeed, he who watches over Israel never tires and never sleeps. The Lord himself watches over you! The Lord stands beside you as your protective shade. The sun will not hurt you by day, nor the moon at night. The Lord keeps you from all evil and preserves your life. The Lord keeps watch over you as you come and go, both now and forever. (Ps. 121:1–8)

3. Brokenness helps us to develop compassion and mercy toward those who are hurting. Suffering serves as a useful purpose; it makes us more sensitive to the needs of people around us. Because we have faced much pain and shame and overcame it, we tend to develop a soft spot in our hearts toward those who are downtrodden and suffering. In this way, God uses our painful experiences to bless the body of Christ through a powerful compassionate ministry to people in dire circumstances (2 Cor. 1:3–7).

4. Brokenness restores spiritual passion and rekindles our first love for the Lord. Broken people emerge from

years of scarcity and want with a greater determination to pour their lives into the service of the master, Jesus Christ. Brokenness renews our hope for the future and helps us to live with eternity in view (Col. 3:1–4).

5. When we are broken, our strength is renewed, we develop resilience to cope with the tough challenges of life, and we overcome them as fly with wings like that of an eagle.

> He gives power to those who are tired and worn out; he offers strength to the weak. Even youths will become exhausted, and young men will give up. But those who wait on the Lord will find new strength. They will fly high on wings like eagles. They will run and not grow weary. They will walk and not faint. (Isaiah 40:29-31)

God gives us new strength, which comes from the Holy Spirit, to accomplish impossible tasks.

6. Brokenness destroys the spirit of bitterness and unforgiveness. Through pain and suffering, God is able to extract the poison of jealousy, hatred, and vindictiveness from our system, which is self-destructive and seeks to destroy the lives of those who harbor it.

7. Brokenness helps pastors and ministers of the gospel to receive a fresh word from the throne room of God and deliver to a world in desperate need of it. It is sad to note that some pastors and gospel ministers do not

have a fresh word from God. A messenger without a message is a confused person. It is wonderful when a servant of God speaks with divine authority and audacity. When you let God do what He wants to do in your life, you will rise up from the ashes of your broken state, with a clear cut message for your world. God will touch your lips with his live coal and your message will burn brightly in the hearts of people world wide.

When Moses finally emerged from the wilderness after forty years of tough times, he went straight to the court of pharaoh, king of Egypt with a divine mandate that shook the foundations of the powerful Egyptian kingdom. Moses' message was so simple that even a little child could understand it: "Let my people go!" Moses drummed that message over and over into the stubborn ears of pharaoh until pharaoh gave up.

8. Brokenness exposes your true enemies and gives you faithful and reliable friends. Remember that patience is the weapon that forces deception to reveal itself. Your trials will force those around you to reveal their true colours. Job's travails forced his three friends to manifest their inner character. It is only with going through tough situations that has the ability to show you the true nature of human beings (both the good and bad sides of human behaviour). And without understanding human nature and discerning your

true friends and real enemies, you cannot proceed with divine wisdom and knowledge in order to fulfil your destiny.

9. Lastly, brokenness forces us to develop addiction for God's presence, which is one of the greatest secrets of a victorious Christian life. When you find yourself in the wilderness, cultivating intimacy with God becomes your primary preoccupation. There is nothing nearly as sweet as cultivating deep intimacy and holy romance with the Holy Spirit through spending hours in daily praise and worship. When you come to a place where you are constant in touch with God, saturated, and overwhelmed by God's fresh touch, nothing else matters.

Instruments of Brokenness

What does God use to break His servants and what happens when a believer refuses to yield to the breaking process and to the leadership of the Holy Spirit? The instrument the Holy Spirit uses to bring us to the point of complete submission to God's will and plan for our lives may differ from one person to another person, depending on our individual set of circumstances and makeup. The choice of which instrument to use to prune, break, and mold us belongs entirely to the Holy Spirit, who is the chief administrative officer in the school of brokenness. The Holy Spirit knows precisely which kind of instrument fits us and for what reason and season. We cannot be too smart for God. We do not choose the instruments for our training and divine preparation; the Holy Spirit chooses the appropriate instruments, and He creates the circumstances and enabling environment for the application of those instruments in our lives. We do not choose trouble; rather, it chooses us. We do not determine how long our problems will last; the Holy Spirit makes the decision on our behalf.

The list of the different kinds of instruments used in the pruning and breaking process is inexhaustible, including instruments such as poverty, false accusation, imprisonment, disability, distressed marriages, prolonged sickness, and failure. Other instruments are widowhood, infidelity, sexual abuse, rape, indebtedness, a wayward child, childlessness, adult singleness, etc. But the question is: what happens when a believer refuses to be broken and prefers to remain in a state of unbrokenness all his life? What are the consequences of the unbroken life?

Symptoms of the Unbroken Life

It is clear from our study of God's Word and basic understanding of the subject of brokenness that rebellion and disobedience attracts severe far-reaching consequences. When we refuse to be broken, the fire of revival upon the altar of our hearts gradually dims and eventually dies out; thus, we have no anointing left. In other words, the oil of the fresh anointing of the Holy Spirit begins to leak out, leaving us spiritually dry, disorganized, and largely insecure. It is never God's will that we should drift away and sink low to the point of losing touch of the freshness of God's presence in our lives and ministry for the Lord. Sadly, there are many pastors and Christian workers serving God without the anointing.

One of the sad stories in the Bible about the unbroken life is the story of King Saul in the Old Testament. Saul broke faith with God and stubbornly refused to surrender to God's dealings (1 Sam. 13:8–14). Saul grew insensitive to the leadership of the Holy Spirit and would not listen to godly counsel through the ministry of the great prophet, Samuel (1 Sam. 15:1–35). As a result, Saul's life began to spin out of control. Saul suffered untold emotional torture, leading to severe depression brought about by guilt and shame. He became unhappy and drifted spiritually away from God. The Holy Spirit left him completely—for good! Now the Spirit of the Lord had left Saul, and the Lord sent a tormenting spirit that filled him, with depression and fear (1 Sam. 16:14). King Saul lost the fire or revival and became insecure. He lost focus and started to pursue young David to kill him. Saul's insecurity and depressive state led him to commit wickedness upon wickedness against people, finally ending his life in misery and shame.

The unbroken life is a curse characterized by obvious symptoms such as insecurity, lust, wickedness, manipulation, secrecy, unforgiveness, unrestrained anger, greed, self-centeredness, jealously, etc.

Key to Brokenness

One critical key to a lifestyle of brokenness is surrender or holy submission (Rom. 12:1–2) to God's divine will. Another vital key is thorough confession and genuine repentance. Repentance brings freedom, favor, fulfilment, and fresh power.

> Oh, what joy for those whose rebellion is forgiven, whose sin is put out of sight! Yes, what joy for those whose record the Lord has cleared of sin, whose lives are lived in complete honesty! When I refused to confess my sin, I was weak and miserably, and I groaned all day long. Day and night your hand of discipline was heavy on me. My strength evaporated like water in the summer heat. Finally, I confessed all my sins to you and stopped trying to hide them. I said to myself, "I will confess my rebellion to the Lord." And you forgave me! All my guilt is gone. Therefore, let all the Godly confess their rebellion to you while there is time that they may not drown in the floodwaters of judgment. For you is my hiding place; you protect me from trouble. You surrounded me with songs of victory. (Ps. 32:1–7)

2

Prayer and Fasting

How DESPERATE ARE you? If you are dead serious about paying the price of revival and fresh anointing and you are ready to do anything in order to experience God in a deeper dimension, then another powerful key, which will reposition you for such a new beginning, is fasting and prayer. Prayer and fasting is the complete withdrawal from all forms of food and other pleasures of life for some period of time for the purpose of concentrated prayer.

Fasting and prayer has value in fanning into flame the fire of revival upon the hearts of God's people. Fasting begins with a hunger for God and for reality. Your desperate hunger and thirst for a new move of God to see the dawning of a new era in your walk with God will automatically drive you on your knees in a desperate cry for mercy and divine intervention.

My first experience of prayer and fasting happened in the mid-1970s when I was still learning to take my first steps to swim in the river of revival and spiritual awakening. I cannot remember anyone teaching me to fast and pray. However, with a deep-seated desire in my heart to know God more and more, I rallied together a small group of young radical Christians and declared three days of prayer and fasting, eating no food and drinking no other liquid but plain water. It was genuine fasting. It was not an easy experience for me and this small discipleship group. We were meeting every day for several hours, praying and interceding for revival in that city. As a result, the Holy Spirit moved. We were also planning three days of a weekend revival meetings, during which we had invited young people from the different secondary schools (high schools) around us. We brought in an anointed guest speaker and a singing group from another city to be with us throughout our weekend revival. Without exaggeration, I can say that the Holy Spirit was poured out mightily in our midst and many precious souls were gloriously saved. The Holy Spirit moved like wildfire, and the students we have invited to the meetings carried the presence of the Holy Spirit back to their various schools. Their lives and their schools were never the same!

It is now more than thirty years since the early days of that divine visitation; however, if you go to that city, you will still find clear evidence of the movement of God in the lives of some of its citizens. Some of these disciples of Christ are going strong in the Lord; some are full-time ministers of the gospel, serving the Lord in different church organizations today.

Food: Mankind's Undoing

One of the worst enemies of mankind is food. It is the unholy craving for food and the fleshly pleasures of life that made man fall into sin (Gen. 3:1–3). When we abuse the privilege of eating and indulge in wanton pleasure and gluttony, we run the risk of losing our spiritual bearing. Food should serve us and not us becoming slaves of our appetite. A lifestyle of continuous fasting and prayer is part of the price you must be willing to pay for wanting to fan into flame fresh revival fires and for desiring to remain on the cutting edge.

In her book, *Korean Miracles*, Reverend Jashil Choi, the late mother-in-law of Dr. David Yonggi Cho—a senior pastor of Yoido Full Gospel church, the world's largest single congregation in Korea—shares some insightful reasons why people over eat. "There are many reasons why people eat excessively."

1.   We eat because it is tasty
2.   We eat because it is nourishing
3.   We eat because it looks delicious

4. We eat for the sake of competition ("I can eat more than you." After eating twenty ice cream servings, a Korean boy became ill and died.)
5. We eat because of greed
6. We overeat because of excessive sampling
7. We eat because of habit
8. We over indulge because others urge us to eat more
9. We eat because of obligation for fear of rejecting hospitability
10. We eat to be sociable
11. We eat because of invitations connected with out official duties
12. We eat because of the fame and reputation of certain foods

Many people consume all kinds of food items without a second thought as though their lives depend on food, rather than God who is the source and giver of life. "We are always interested in eating. The subject of food captures our attention. In addition to our regular meals, we crave delicious delicate snacks and fancy desserts. Many people live to eat. However, there is a much higher dimension of living. By fasting and prayer, the Holy Spirit can work through us in a more powerful degree. Even in this ultra scientific generation we may see, hear and experience a great varsity of miracles, signs and wonders."

Types of Fasting

There are only three types of fasting in human experience:

1. **Absolute Fast**

    This category of fasting is also referred to as nothing-at-all fast because throughout its duration, you eat nothing and drink nothing, including ordinary water and all forms of liquid, until the period of the fasting is over. This is the kind of fasting that Queen Esther ordered for all the Jews in Shushan, capital city of Persia, during a season of emergency (Esth. 4:15–17). It is the toughest and the most dramatic form of fasting and is known to produce the quickest results, perhaps due to the degree and intensity of desperation that accompanies it.

    The *absolute fast* is tough because without water or liquids in the body during the first two or three days, the pain and discomfort in various parts of the body are unbearable. The desire to eat food is intense, especially for those who are doing the fast for the first time. Almost in all cases, people undertake the absolute fast under desperate times. They hold on to God and would not let go with a sense of desperation and reckless abandon until heaven responds. However, based on health grounds, it may not be advisable to make a habit out of it because the body needs water.

Due to the danger and health hazards associated with dehydration (loss of water in the body), believers who undertake this fast should consider limiting it to only two or three days at a time as a general rule.

2. Normal Fast

This is the water-only fast because throughout its duration, only extraordinarily clean or purified water is consumed. With proper water intake on a consistent basis, a believer may fast for a period of seven to fifteen days successfully. You drink plenty of water on the first day of your fast and follow it up by drinking water on a consistent basis. Water serves as your food, body cleanser, and restorer of lost energy. Medically, the normal fast is highly recommended for your health and longevity because during this time, water flushes toxins and poison out of your system. The digestive tract and the organs of your body go on a break and shut down for rest and recuperation. Then you are able to enjoy maximum healing from certain diseases.

However, on the day you are starting your normal fast, remember to empty your bowels of waste material; since waste material left in your digestive tract will translate into poison, causing damage to your brain and the vital organs of your body and endangering your health. Locate a simple method of empting your bowels and apply it appropriately anytime you plan a normal fast.

3. **Partial Fast**

Another way by which God's people can experience fresh anointing and obtain supernatural breakthrough is through a *partial fast*. It is important to remember that all other forms of fasting outside of *absolute* and *normal fasts*, fall within the category of a *partial fast*. The partial fast, which is a regulated fast based on our personal convenience and circumstances, gives you room for an extended time and still carry out daily work schedule.

There are different expressions of a partial fast among God's people worldwide. a few of which are listed below:

- *Vegetables Only fast.* While in Bablyon on exile, Daniel and his three friends refused to eat the king's food and delicacies on religious grounds, preferring to live on vegetables and water (Daniel 1:8–20).

- *Fasting Choice Food.* In Daniel Chapter 10, Daniel refrained from eating choice food for three weeks including drinking wine and the use of fragrant oil because these were signs of feasting and pleasure. Daniel refrained from these choice food in order to seek the face of God (Daniel 10:1–21).

- *Juice Fasting.* Some believers in America and other western nations prefer to live on water and the juice of organic fruits throughout the duration of their fast. Juice fasting is highly recommended due to its health benefits, including healing from certain diseases.
- *Fasting Two Meals a Day.* Here you refrain from having breakfast and lunch and you eat at 6.00 p.m. In other words, you eat one good meal with fruits once every twenty-four hours. If you happen to be on a long fast of this category, remember to drink water during the course of each day to prevent weakness and dehydration.
- *Fasting One Meal a Day.* Many Christians have discovered that fasting one meal a day or skipping breakfast daily has helped them to maintain focus and position themselves for divine intervention. "Repeatedly overeating at breakfast time can cause you to drag through the morning feeling mental strain and not at all in full attention. To have a keen sense of judgment is difficult, but many people have found by fasting breakfast and spending the time in prayer, they have a clear head, are at full attention, and have a good sense of judgment. If possible, fast one meal a day from time to time. Through fasting one meal a day, many people stay healthy and enjoy long life. Among

my friends and family, there are many these days who fast one meal a day. Fasting is profitable 3 in maintaining physical health"

Benefits of Fasting

Many people are hesitant and afraid to fast. But if they get to know the overwhelming benefits of fasting, they will change their minds and begin to adopt fasting as a lifestyle. There are many benefits of fasting. Let us consider a few of these benefit.

- Fasting helps God's people to walk in the fullness and freshness of the presence and power of the Holy Spirit. Many Christians are living defeated lives; they have lost their first love and their cutting edge. The fire of revival that was once burning brightly in their lives and services for God has diminished. In some cases, the fresh touch of God is no longer present. The fire is dead. Many worthy causes for God's kingdom have died, and the vision bearers have forsaken their previous calling simply because the price of the ministry was to be too much to bear. Now is the time for divine restoration. This comes through prayer and fasting.
- Fasting is one of the greatest secrets of spiritual power. With a good fasting routine, we become a conductor of God's power. The anointing that

breaks every yoke comes through fasting and prayer. Pastors, church workers, and ministers of the gospel should always remember to prepare their messages (sermons) on their knees in prayer and fasting to be able to preach under a new level of anointing in their ministries. Without disciplined prayer and a fasting lifestyle, not much can be accomplished for God and His kingdom. The kind of preaching and teaching of God's Word, which causes dry bones to hear your voice and respond to your orders, is not cheap; it comes with a price.

- Fasting is the key to miracles. When you become a diligent student in the school of fasting, signs and wonders will follow you. Sometimes those miracles will show up in little things and big things and, subsequently, in an amazing fashion. You will see the finger of God in your daily walk (Exod. 14:13–14). Friends, if you truly desire miracles and you want to prosper, start praying and fasting. Be consistent, be determined, be focused, and God will visit you.

- Fasting breaks down our senses, conquering our flesh and the natural desire of our lives and causing us to be more sensitive to hear the voice of God. Fasting is an introduction into the realms of the spirit and a doorway to the operation of the Holy Spirit in the lives of the God's servants. To some, the Christian life is boring and dull. Our ears are full of hearing from

God. God no longer speaks. Life is no longer exciting. There is nothing new happening in the inner recesses of their hearts to excite them. Our numerous religious activities, conferences, conventions, seminars, and gospel crusades cannot fill the empty void in our hearts. But when we get desperate and there is hunger in our hearts to know God, something happens. God shows up and life begins to get exciting again. When was the last time you heard the voice of God? There is a general fallacy today that only men and women of God can hear from Him and get direction for their lives. Hearing and discerning God's voice is not the privilege of a few individuals. God has no favorite. You too can hear the voice of God—that is, if you are willing to pay the price.

- Fasting helps us to slow down, stop talking, and learn to listen more. Through fasting, God will give you a garment of praise instead of the spirit of heaviness (Is. 61:3). Fasting inspires boldness, courage, and fearlessness with an audacious spirit to take certain steps in order to bring about our breakthrough and enhance our growth and maturity—steps that we may never be able to take under normal circumstances.
- Fasting sharpens our focus and gives us a new mission for a brand new beginning. As the body gets weak during fasting, our senses become sharper and sharper so that we are able to see and perceive mysteries and

fresh revelation from God's Word. Fasting prepares you for possible future spiritual battles, which you may not yet sense in your life. When the Holy Spirit calls you to fast it may be a *trap* or maybe God is preparing you for what is ahead. Fasting prepares you to face impending danger in the strength and power of the Holy Spirit.

> The Lord looks down from heaven and sees the whole human race. From his throne, he observes all who live on the earth. He made their hearts, so he understands everything they do. The best-equipped army cannot save a king, nor is great strength enough to save a warrior. Don't count on your warhorse to give you victory—for all is strength, it cannot save you. But the Lord watches over those who fear him, those who rely on his unfailing love. He rescues them from death and keeps them alive in times of famine. We depend on the Lord alone to save us. Only he can help us, protecting us like a shield. In him our hearts rejoice, for we are trusting in his holy name. Let your unfailing love surround us, Lord, for our hope is in your alone. (Ps. 33:13–22)

- Fasting helps us to develop resilience. It is not easy to cope with tough challenges and take a stand for Jesus in the face of adversity, in the face of fierce opposition, and in the face of persecution.

- Fasting forces your personality to mature. When you fast diligently, you command respect in the presence of your spouse and family members. There is peace and harmony in the home.
- Fasting will reposition you for double anointing and for the realization of supernatural power. Fasting gives believers' special grace to work for God. Fasting will take you to the next level of God's power, grace, and mercy.
- Fasting helps us to adopt a more healthy lifestyle and gives us physical, mental, and psychological healing. In the book, *Fasting Made Easy*, Dr. Don Colbert, a medical doctor, shares extensively on the health benefits of a good fast. Don Colbert recommends the *Juice Fast*.

> In my experience as a physician, I have seen heart disease, diabetes, hypertension, arthritis, chronic fatigue, and many other serious diseases reversed as my patients cleanse their bodies from toxins through fasting. In addition, detoxifying your body through fasting can also help rid you of excess weight if you are overweight or even obese. Not only will you feel better and live longer as you remove toxins from your body, but you will look better as well. Eyes become bright and skin glows as you enjoy the vitality of higher energy levels. Though fasting may seem like a "sacrifice"

at first, I want you to understand the wonderful potential it has for enhancing your health and helping you to maintain a healthy lifestyle.

One of the most vital and most essential organs in the body is the liver. The liver performs multiple functions in the body, including filtering your blood to remove toxins, viruses, bacteria, and yeast. So the liver acts as a filter in the body. Fasting is absolutely necessary because it gives your body time to rest and regain itself. During fasting, the liver undergoes the process of rest, detoxification, and self-cleaning.

> Your liver may get overloaded with toxins from our food and water, parasites, toxins in the air, toxins in the home or workplace, and from free radicals produced internally in the liver by the detoxification process itself. Like dust and dirt that accumulate in your air filter, these toxins make the liver work too hard; eventually, it cannot function efficiently. That is why fasting becomes important to allow the liver to rest and be able to catch up with its cleaning duties.

So periodically, you need to fast in order to give your digestive tract, your liver, and the rest of the body time for rest and recuperation. Without this, the organs of the body may spark and may one day break down due to overloading with toxins and overwork! The *water-only fast* or the *juice fast* is excellent to give the body sufficient time for rest, rejuvenation and cleaning. Furthermore, fasting gives shopping housewives holiday and fasting helps them to break the circle of cooking, doing dishes and. When we all fast as a family, there is harmony, peace and rest.

- Fasting is all-gain with nothing to lose.

Fasting Retreat

The kind of fasting you choose each time you desire to wait on the Lord (Is. 40:31) and the duration (length) of your fast are all subject to the leadership of the Holy Spirit and your personal conviction. However, as much as possible, seek to master shorter fasts over a period of time before undertaking the fifteen-, thirty-, and forty-day fasts or even a prolonged partial fast.

One experience of fasting that I have enjoyed over the years of my Christian walk and service of the Lord, which I wish to strongly recommend to you, is what I refer to as a fasting retreat. A *fasting retreat* is a season when you withdraw from people and public life to seek God's face in quietness, meditation, and prayer in a solitary place away from your home. Fasting retreats do not come by easily due to the difficulty of locating an appropriate place for your prayer and fasting time.

In South Korea, Christians have built many prayer retreat centers (known as prayer mountains) scattered all over the country, where people retreat to wrestle with God for supernatural breakthrough. Some of the prayer mountains have *grottos* (prayer caves) for individual prayer. In that way, many believers in South Korea have discovered the secret of locking themselves up in a prayer cave for days—sometimes even weeks—and would not let ut until heaven responds to their desperate cry. In many parts of the world, these special prayer retreat centers are not available, and many believers find it difficult to locate a place that is reserved purposely for seeking the face of the Lord.

In the city where I used to live in Nigeria, some churches and Christian organizations have built guest houses, which are being used to accommodate guests who come into the city to attend various Christian conferences and seminars for a certain reasonable fee. I found that these guest houses are quite suitable for my prayer and fasting retreats. Over the years, I have utilized them as my fasting retreat centers. For those who are pastors, missionaries, evangelists, and church leaders planning to go on a fasting retreat at least once in a year, it is indispensable to be hearing from God and receiving clear directions for the future. Some believers go on a fasting retreat right at the beginning of every year so that they can bask in the glow of God's presence, surrender all to Jesus, and invite the Holy Spirit to take charge of the rest of the year. For me, fasting retreats have helped me to hear the voice of God during defining moments and take accurate steps on a number of vital and sensitive issues in my ministry. I have done fasting retreats of three to seven days with either *absolute* or a *normal* fast a few times in our home; but in most cases, I go to a retreat place somewhere away from our home. For instance, after spending seven days alone with God on a *water-only fasting* retreat, I leave my retreat place with a powerful assurance of God's presence with an incredible peace in my soul. Often, God shows up, He gives me dreams and visions, and fresh revelation from His Word. God gives me definite miracles.

If you get definite with God, God will get definite with you. God is faithful. He is no respecter of persons. Even though three or seven days on a normal fast may seem like as short fast for some people who is accustomed to prolonged fasting, for me, its significance lies in the fact that it is three or seven days and nights of solitude, seclusion, and secret private prayer alone with God in holy romance with the Holy Spirit in quiet solitude, meditation, and prayer.

When you are preparing to go on a fasting retreat, remember to pray, commit to seeing it through, and ask God for wisdom concerning what to prepare in order to ensure that you are going to spend uninterrupted quality time with the Almighty God. Remember to carry along with you your Bible, a journal, and some good reading material to keep you busy throughout the duration of your time. I like reading biographies and stories of the exploits of men and women in the past centuries so I make sure to carry with me some inspiring biography. As I read a biography and spend time studying my Bible, I also take down notes in my journal, which I keep and guard jealously for future reference.

Learn to take a long walk each day during your prayer and fasting retreat. Walking a long distance and praying is pleasurable. One fasting retreat done in the right spirit can change your life forever.

Breaking a Fast

In breaking a fast, it is important to remember that the degree of willpower and discipline, which the Holy Spirit helped you to apply to be able to begin and complete a fast successfully, will be greatly needed to help you walk through the process of breaking your fast without causing harm to your body. As a general principle, the number of days it took you to complete your fast will be the same number of days you will need to take in order to work your way into eating a normal diet of food again. If you become complacent, insensitive, and allow gluttony to take over your natural appetite for food, you may likely suffer and may be tempted to regret the entire fasting process. Remember that during fasting, the digestive tract shuts down, shrinking in size, and the tissues around the rectum becoming soft and sensitive. Your stomach may not reject what you consume immediately following your fast, but if it is solid food and you have been on a normal or juice fast for sometime, you may likely have difficulty eliminating any waste material from your digestive tract. In seeking to break your fast, begin by taking pap, softly cooked vegetables, and juice. Do not introduce any hard substance into your stomach following a fast.

Believers who desire to know more about some helpful tips regarding the subject of prayer and fasting should endeavour to read other books on this important Christian discipline. As you gain deeper insight on the subject of fasting, remember that sustaining the freshness of the presence of the Holy Spirit and remaining on the cutting edge is not cheap. Pastors and church leaders must learn to cultivate discipline in this area and seek to become diligent students in the school of fasting if their ministries for the Lord must become relevant in these challenging times. One of the greatest secrets of fresh anointing and remaining on the cutting edge lies in the practice of prayer and fasting.

Brother Jentezen Franklin has summed it up beautifully: Throughout the history of the Christian church, God has raised up men and women who are willing to dedicate their lives to Him and diligently seek Him through fasting and prayer. Long seasons of fasting are credited for launching such revivals as seen by Even Roberts in Laos, who fasted and prayed for thirteen months for that country. Healing evangelists like John Alexander Dowie, John G. Lake, Maria Woodworth Etter, Smith Wigglesworth, and Kathryn Kuhlman all understood the tremendous power of faith in operation throughout their ministries."

3

Welcome the Holy Spirit

BE SHARP AND sensitive to the Holy Spirit. One of the secrets of fresh anointing is learning to welcome the Holy Spirit into your life. You cannot grow with limitless capacity and soar to great heights without developing sensitivity to the Holy Spirit. The Holy Spirit is your most prized asset or possession in life. There is no gift you have in your possession more precious than the gift of the Holy Spirit, the third person of the Trinity. He is your best friend, your confidante, and your senior partner in the kingdom. Without His blessing and favour, your life will amount to nothing.

> So he answered and said to me: "This is the word of the Lord to Zerubbabel: Not by might nor by power, but by My Spirit" says the Lord of hosts. (Zech. 4:6).

The touch, the blessing, the grace, and the favour that the Holy Spirit bestows upon a believer's life are all you need to succeed in this life. It is only through God's awesome Spirit that anything of lasting value can be accomplished for God and His kingdom.

What we need to do to keep the fire of revival burning brightly upon the altar of our hearts is learning to develop great sensitively to the person and leadership of the Holy Spirit. The key is to welcome the Holy Spirit and let Him have His way in every aspect of your life. Let the Holy Spirit take charge of your life and let it guide you. The apostles of Christ succeeded marvelously in ministry and were on the cutting edge of the gospel because they discovered the key that unlocks the door of fresh anointing, which is being sharp and sensitive to the marching orders of the Holy Spirit. Learn to welcome the Holy Spirit and be sensitive to His leading.

Paul and Silas planted a great church in Phillippi and in all of Asia Minor among the Gentiles because of their high sensitivity to the Holy Spirit. Now when they had gone through Phrgia and the region of Galatia, they were forbidden by the Holy Spirit to preach in Asia. After they had come to Mysia, they tried to go into Bithynia but the Spirit did not permit them. So passing by Mysia, they came down to Troas. A vision appeared to Paul in the night. A man of Macedonia stood and pleaded with him, saying,"Come over to Macedonia and help us." Now after he had seen the vision, "immediately we sought to go to Macedonia, concluding that the Lord had called us to preach the gospel to them. Therefore, sailing from Troas, we ran a straight course to Samothrace, and the next day to came to Neapolis, and from there to Philippi, which is the foremost city of that part of Mecadinia, a colony, we were staying in that city for some days (Acts 16:6–12).

The Holy Spirit is our Divine guide, the lord of the harvest and commander in chief of the armies of heaven. How dare we, mere mortals, disobey His marching orders. How dare we refuse to carry out His instruction! It was the Holy Spirit who championed and actually launched the first missionary evangelistic outreach to the Gentiles during the early days of the apostles. Paul and Barnabas were the first people to be sent out to the mission field because the church in Antioch listened to the voice of the Holy Spirit.

> Now in the church that was at Antioch there were certain prophets and teachers: Barnabas, Simeon who was called Nigir, Lucius of Cyrene, Manach who has been brought up with Herod the Tetrarch and Saul. As they ministered to the Lord and fasted, the Holy Spirit said, "Now separate to me Barnabas and Saul for the work to which I have called them." Then, having fasted and prayed and laid hands on them, they sent them away. So being sent out by the Holy Spirit, they went down to Seleucia, and from there they sailed to Cyprus. And when they arrived in Salamis, they preached the word of God in the synagogues of the Jews; they also had John as their assistant. (Acts 13:1–5)

Do not offend the Holy Spirit. But someone may ask, "How can a Christian develop great sensitivity to the Holy Spirit and walk in the freshness of God's presence on a day to day basis?" In Ephesians 4:30, the Bible warns us not offend or cause the Holy Spirit sorrow. How does a believer offend (hurt) the Holy Spirit? "And do not bring sorrow to God's Holy Spirit by the way you live. Remember, He is the one who has identified you as he own, guaranteeing that you will be saved on the day of redemption" (Eph. 4:30).

What does a Christian do or not do that makes the Holy Spirit sad? What happens when we grow insensitive to the Holy Spirit and allow indifference, familiarity complex, and complacency to creep into our relationship with the Holy Spirit? Firstly, the Holy Spirit is grieved (becomes sad) when we refuse to surrender and yield our lives to Him. The fresh touch of God's presence rests on us when we welcome the Holy Spirit and let Him have His way in every aspect of our lives.

> I beseech you therefore, brethren, by the mercies of God, that you present your bodies a living sacrifice, holy, acceptable to God, which is your reasonable service. And do not be conformed to this world, but be transformed by the renewing of your mind, that you may prove what is that good and acceptable and perfect will of God. (Rom. 12:1–2)

As a gentle being, the Holy Spirit will not force His way; but if we surrender all to Him and let Him take charge, our lives will take on a new meaning. Let me ask you: have you laid your all on the altar of sacrifice? Does Jesus have full control of your life or are you still playing games (hide-and-seek) with the Holy Spirit?

Secondly, the Holy Spirit is offended (hurt and wounded) and will not operate freely when we rebel against His will and outright disobey His marching orders. Remember that God was not happy with King Saul, the first king of the nation of Israel. When King Saul consistently rebelled and disobeyed God's divine instructions (1 Sam. 13:8–15, 15:22–23). Because of Saul's rebellion, God rejected him as the king of Israel. As a result, God's presence was withdrawn from King Saul. The Holy Spirit left Saul's life and ministry, and from then on, King Saul was on his own without a divine cover! The worse thing that can happen to any person on the face of this planet is to live a life totally devoid of divine cover. How can a believer survive without God's presence, God's touch, and God's favor? It is no wonder that without the anointing, King Saul's ministry ended in such tragic failure, great shame, and disgrace. The mystery of it all is though the Holy Spirit left King Saul, he continued to rule as the king of Israel for more than thirty years, carrying out his ministry!

Thirdly, the Holy Spirit is hurt when we do God's work with unholy hands. Another person who completely lost the anointing and fresh touch of God's presence on his life and ministry through sexual immorality is Samson (Judges 16). Samson was not careful; he was not sensitive to his calling or sensitive to the Holy Spirit who called him. Samson did not apply discipline and he was not prepared to pay the price for sustaining the precious and rare anointing on his life. Like some pastors, Christian workers, and church leaders today, perhaps Samson thought he could still carry out a powerful revival and evangelistic ministry with signs and wonders and at the same time, satisfy the natural cravings of his flesh. From one moral compromise to another, Samson gradually lost focus and bearing. His enemies, the Philistine warlords, understood his weak point, and they set a trap for him by hiring a loose woman, Deliliah, to entice him and consequently discover the secret of his strength. Samson descended so low in his moral choice that the enemy got to him.

> When Deliliah saw that he had told her all his heart, she sent and called for the lords of the Philistines, saying. "Come up once more, for he has told my all his heart." So the lord of the Philistines came up to her and brought the money in their hand. Then she lulled him to sleep on her knees, and called for a man and had him shave off the seven locks on his head. Then she began to torment him, and his strength left him. And she said, "The Philistines are upon you, Samson!" so he awoke from his sleep and said. "I will gout as before at other times, and shake myself free!" But he did not know that the Lord had departed from

him. Then the Philistines took him and put out his
eyes, and brought him to Gaza. They bound him with
bronze fetters, and he came a grinder in prison. (Judg.
16:18–21)

If we are truly serious about walking in the freshness of
divine anointing and power and we mean business in seeking
divine approval rather than human applause, then we must
hate sexual impurity in all its forms and different aspects of
its manifestation. God is Holy. Sexual sin is a curse!

> God wants you to be holy so you should keep clear of
> all sexual sin. You will control your body and live in
> holiness and honor not in lustful passion as the pagans
> do, in their ignorance of God and his way us. Never
> cheat a Christian brother in this matter by taking his
> wife, for the Lord avenges all such sins, as we have
> solemnly warned you before. God has called us to be
> holy, not to live impure lives. Anyone who refuses to
> live by these rules is not disobeying human rules but
> is rejecting God's who give his Holy Spirit to you. (1
> Thess. 4:3–8)

Another thing which makes the Holy Spirit angry is
lying and deceit. Ananias and Sapphira fell into this trap.
As a result, the Holy Spirit was extremely displeased with
them and instantly, they lost their lives. They died and gave
up the ghost (Acts 5:1–11). Also, the Holy Spirit is grieved

and offended when we dare to touch God's glory. We must learn to walk in humility, giving all the glory to God for all our successes, achievements, and accomplishments in life. God does not share His glory with people (Is. 42:8). We need to constantly remember that we are what were purely by the grace of God. Subtly, Ananias and Sapphira dared to touch God's glory through their deceit, especially since Barnabas' donation of a piece of land as a gift (Acts 4:36–37). Ananias and Sapphira conceived a lie to manipulate and mislead the church. Could it be that by their deceit, Ananias and Sapphira were seeking to gain the approval of the apostles? The Holy Spirit was quick to detect both deceit and wicked pride and the Holy Spirit dealt with it decisively with capital punishment, lest the devil should gain access and infiltrate the ranks of the early church.

Lastly, the Holy Spirit is saddened by our bitterness and unforgiving spirit. We hurt the Holy Spirit when we harbour malice and we refuse to forgive one another.

> And do not grieve the Holy Spirit of God, by whom you were sealed for the day of redemption. Let all bitterness, wrath, anger, clamor an evil speaking be put away from you, with all malice. And be kind to one another, tender hearted forgiving one another, even as God in Christ forgive you. (Eph. 4:30–32)

4

Early Morning Prayer

Breakfast of Champions

THE EARlY MORNing prayer is the breakfast of champions. If you truly desire to rekindle your first love for God and want to bask in the sunshine of God's burning love, you must endeavour to get up in the early hours every day to pray. Many of God's servants prefer to feast in God's Word and prayer in the secret place before venturing out with their day-to-day routine. Finding grace in the secret place in the early hours has proved to be one of the greatest secrets of strength through the centuries for serious-minded believers and the deeply committed ministers of the gospel.

It was Oswald J. Smith, a missionary statesman and senior pastor of peoples church, Toronto, Canada, who said that: "A pastor's power for service will rise or fall in direct proportion to how faithfully he spends his time alone with God." John Wesley (1703–1791), the founder of the Methodist church, discovered the secret of a successful fruit-abiding evangelistic gospel ministry. It was said that John Wesley used to get up between the hours of four to six in the morning to pray and mediate on God's word every day for sixty yeas of his life. No wonder his terrific preaching on horseback brought great revival to England and America during the eighteenth century.

Oswald Chambers advises God's people to develop the habit of seeking God's face in the morning: "Get into the habit of dealing with God about everything. Unless in the first waking moment of the day you learn to fling the door wide back and let God in, you will work on a wrong level all day; but swing the door wide open and pray to your Father in secret; and every public thing will be stamped with the presence of God."

Dr. David Yonggi Cho is the senior pastor emeritus of Yoido Full Gospel Church, the world's largest single congregation of 760,000 members in Seoul, Korea. Dr. Cho shares a personal testimony of what the early morning prayer means to him and how seeking God's face through his devotional time. He has found strength to minister to a large church with so many challenges.

Many people ask me how long I pray each day. When they learn that I pray one to three hours a day, they are interested to know how I can manage to take that time when my responsibilities are so heavy. Part of my three hours is my personal devotional time communing and fellowshipping with the Holy Spirit, and part is my regular prayer time. Actually, I cannot afford to pray less. The heavier my responsibilities are, the more I must stay in close fellowship with the Holy Spirit for His guidance and anointing when preaching. This has been proven in my life many, many times.

I have found that the early hours of the morning are best for personal devotions because I am rested and the presence of the Lord has created a desire for prayer. No matter where I am—at home in Korea or abroad in other countries in a Church Growth Seminar or gospel crusade—I usually begin my prayer time at 4.30 a.m. and pray until 6.30 a.m. I always begin my prayer time with worship aloud. I pray aloud so that I can hear myself and that prevents me from dozing off to sleep. After I have ministered unto the Lord, then I begin my regular prayer time. I have a list of prayer requests that I take with me to prayer, and I pray for each one. I pray for my pastors, elders, deacons and deaconesses, staff members and my family, one by one. I ask God to bless their ministries that day and to meet their personal needs. At the conclusion, I spend time waiting before the Lord so that I may hear from Him.

> Now I cannot say that is easy to pray each time I
> go apart for prayer. But consistent prayer makes me
> sensitive to the power and presence of the Holy Spirit
> and that is wonderful. It also makes me sensitive to the
> hindering spirit, which might be present to discourage
> me from praying. But as I persist in worshipping the
> Lord with thanksgiving and praise, I always break
> through the barriers into the presence of the Lord.

If you desire to maintain the power and freshness of the presence of the Holy Spirit in your life and Christian service, you would need to develop a strong determination to pray and make enormous personal sacrifice to remain on the cutting edge.

Rekindling your first love for God on a consistent basis as you advance in age, facing diverse challenges in your marriage and work life is not a cheap matter. Staying on the cutting edge requires that you must make up you remind to build an altar for God, or perhaps you may need to repair your broken altar.

Jesus, Our Perfect Model

Jesus Christ is our perfect model in all matters relating to faith and practice. From our study of God's Word, we have discovered that rising up to seek the face of the Lord in the morning was a great secret of strength for our Lord and Master, Jesus Christ. Even though, He is the Son of God,

Jesus applied the rugged discipline of prayer and worship in the early hours of the day during His earthly ministry in order to keep the anointing fresh and the fire of revival burning brightly in His own life and service.

> The next morning Jesus awoke long before day break and went out alone into the wilderness to pray. Later Simon and the others went out to find him. They said, "Everyone is asking for you", But he replied, "we must go on to other towns as well, and I will preach to them, too, because that is why I came", so he travelled throughout the region of Galilee, preaching in the synagogues and expelling demons from many people." (Mark 1:35–39)

From the above portion of scripture, we notice that the personal devotional life of prayer and worship was a top priority in Jesus's life and ministry. Jesus established a pattern of prayer, which should guide us today; that is, ministry to God must come first before ministry to other people. This pattern of prayer as demonstrated by Jesus during His earthly ministry is one of the greatest secrets of strength of all great men and women through the centuries. King David was one person who derived strength and great inspiration from his personal devotional time, especially in the early morning. "O Lord, hear me as I pray; pay attention to my groaning. Listen to my cry for help, my king and my God, for I will never pray to anyone but you. Listen to my voice in the morning,

Lord. Each morning, I bring my requests to you and wait expectedly" (Ps. 5:1–3).

Someone has correctly observed that, "The secret of a close relationship with God is to pray to him earnestly each morning. In the morning, our minds are more free from problems, and then, we can commit the whole day to God. Regular communication" helps any friendship and is certainly necessary for a strong relationship with God. We need to communicate with him daily. Do you have a regular time to pray and read God's word?"

Nevertheless, some Christians are asking: "What are the benefits of the early morning prayer?

Benefits of the Early Morning Prayer

There are several benefits and blessings to a Christian who takes his early morning devotional time seriously. First of all, early morning prayer is a time of extravagant praise and worship.

When I enter my closet (my private prayer place) during the early hours of the day, I usually take some time to worship God and sing songs of praise to Him (often, out loud). If you were my next-door neighbor, you will likely hear my voice worshipping and praising God early in the morning. It is not my practice to read my Bible during morning devotions; I read my Bible at other times during the day. Once in my prayer closet, I sit comfortably on a chair with a hard surface.

I usually begin my prayer by spending considerable time (between thirty minutes to one hour) in praise and worship. I have discovered over time that praise sets the right tune for my prayer time, creating a conducive atmosphere for the divine presence of the Holy Spirit. Extravagant praise to God out loud helps me to concentrate. Anointed praise and worship is the doorway into the inner sanctuary, the throne room of the Most High God, where we are privileged to dine with the Holy Spirit and the Holy Trinity on matters of eternal destiny.

During my time of praise and worship and intercessory prayer time, I keep my eyes completely closed in order to avoid distraction and somehow relish the intense aura of God's presence. By the time I am through praising, worshipping, and praying for about an hour or more, I sense a fresh touch of God's presence in my life, which lingers on during the day. The thing is, worship creates the right atmosphere for prayer. I have discovered that it is not easy to start praying immediately or putting myself in the right mode for prayer. Worship is the key that unlocks the door to the free flow of God's presence and helps me conquer distractions and wandering thoughts, especially at the beginning of my devotional time with the Holy Spirit. Praise and worship works like magic; it brings God's presence into our lives faster than anything else that I know of. The reasons is simple:

"Praise is where God lives. It is His permanent address. Praise is His home element. He is at home in praise. He is 'great and greatly to be praised' (Psalm 48:1). This settles one of the vast mysteries which accompanies praise. Why is it that when we praise the Lord things change so rapidly? Why does healing come on the wings of praise? Why do human emotions undergo such transition when praise is the choice? How are we to account for these things which accompany praise?" The answer is simple. "While God is everywhere, he is not everywhere manifested. He is at home in praise and being at home, He manifest himself best as God! When you and I choose to make God at home through praise, we invite him to act at home." When God is at home in praise, he does what he wants to do."

Secondly, another benefit of the early morning prayer is that it is a place of thorough confession, true repentance, and a broken spirit. The early morning prayer is a time of spiritual cleansing when we get a correct assessment our worth before God and before people. A Christian who does not spend sufficient time with God or cultivate deep intimacy and holy romance with God, especially during the early hours of each day, is full of false confidence. The reality is, we may never know the depth of our own sins or even of our own pain until we enter our prayer closet, the secret place of God's presence. While we are sitting in the secret place and the glory of God begins to shine on us, exposing our unworthiness, we fall on our face before God, confessing and repenting of all known and unknown sins. Often, we leave God's presence with the assurance of forgiveness by the blood of Christ and freedom in our spirit to do the perfect will of God for our lives.

Thirdly, the early morning prayer is ideal for receiving direction and focus for each day's unknown challenges. Praying during the early hours of the day helps us to discern God's will and receive the anointing to make correct decisions and take accurate steps. When we enter our prayer closets and spend time in God's presence, His glory rubs off on us. God speaks to us through His gentle still small voice, showing us specific steps to take and what to avoid. No Christian dares to miss out of guidance and direction to cultivate deep intimacy with the Lord by developing the rugged discipline of meeting God every day in prayer, worship, and Bible meditation on a consistent basis.

Also, another blessing that comes from lingering in God's presence early in the morning is the victory, which comes as a result of prayer warfare. It is in our prayer closets that we receive grace and supernatural ability to wrestle through many critical issues on our mind. The Bible makes it abundantly clear that perfect peace and a calm spirit (devoid of worry, fear, vindictiveness, jealousy, hot temper, gossip, unforgiving spirit, etc.) come because we have prayed for breakthrough.

> Don't worry about anything, instead, pray about everything. Tell God what you need, and thank him for all he has done. If you do this, you will experience god's peace, which is far more wonderful than the

human man can understand. His peace as you live in
Christ Jesus. (Phil. 4:6–7)

In the morning, we learn to tell God precisely what is on
our mind, how we feel about certain issues, and what we desire
that He does for us. In this way, we are able to transfer our
battles to God. It is wonderful to watch God intervene and
work out miracles, bringing sanity into a terrible confusion in
a ways that beat human imagination. God is a great promise
keeper and a wonderful way maker!

The following poem by Raph Cushman (from an unknown
source) will help us to possess a better understanding of how
God moves swiftly to intervene and give us victory in the
midst of turbulent storms when we dare to seek His face in
prayer and Bible meditation.

In the Morning

I met God in the morning
When my day was at its best
And His presence came like sunrise
Like a glory in my breast.

All day the presence lingered
All day long He stayed with me
And we sailed with perfect calmness
O'er a very troubled sea

Other ships were blown and battered
Other ships were sore distressed
But the winds that seemed to drive them
Brought to us a peace and rest

Then I thought of other mornings
With a keen remorse of mind
When I, too, had loosed the moorings
With the presence left behind.

So I think I know the secret
Learned from many a troubled way
You must seek God in the morning
If you want Him through the day

5

Prompt Obedience

Prompt Obedient is the Key

PROMPT AND UNQUESTIONABLE obedience to the marching orders of the Holy Spirit is a great key secret of the abiding fresh presence of God in the lives of His people. God does not only demand obedience, He blesses prompt obedient. Your quick and spontaneous obedience is what God is looking for in a man or woman He desires to use to accomplish His eternal purposes on earth. Without prompt obedience, you may never be able to move to the next level of promotion, progress, and maturity in the spiritual realm. Obeying God's voice instantly and doing God's will immediately takes you from where you are to where you should be, as far as God's agenda and program for your life is concerned.

God will not bless or prosper you until He has tested you sufficiently in many ways over a period of time for the genuineness of your love for Him and the promptness of your obedience. God blesses those who obey him promptly. In other words, the degree of your prompt obedience, determines the degree of your promotion; because prompt obedience is the common denominator of true promotion. When God asks a person to do a challenging or difficult task, it may be a setup. He is about to move that person to a new level of progress. The test always precedes the blessing so that we might not be tempted to touch God's glory. Prompt obedience is the key to fresh fire.

Abraham Obeyed Promptly

Abraham was called the father of faith because he was known for his prompt, unquestionable obedience, and strong faith. Abraham was called by God to leave his comfort zone, his birth place, his own people, and his beloved country to start a new life in an entirely unknown destination—and he obeyed promptly!

> Then the Lord told Abram, "Leave your country, your relatives and your father's house, and go to the land that I will show you. I will cause you to become the father of a great nation. I will bless you and make you

famous, and I will make you a blessing to others. I will bless those who bless you and curse those who curse you. All the families of the earth will be blessed through you." So Abram departed as the Lord had instructed him, and Lot went with him. Abram was seventy five years when he let Haran. He took his wife, Sarai, his nephew Lot, and his wealth his livestock and all the people who had joined his household at Haran and finally arrived in Canaan. Traveling through Canaan, they came to a place near Shechem and set up camp beside the oak at Moreh. At that time, the area was inherited by Canaanites. (Gen. 12:1–6)

When God told Abraham to leave the comfort and security of his present position against all odds, Abraham promptly obeyed. He did not delay. He took off and headed toward Canaan as quickly as he could in direct obedience to divine mandate!

The question is, how quick do you respond whenever God speaks to you? Remember that delaying what the Holy Spirit has explicitly told you to do could be disastrous. Delay opens the door to rationalization, which leads to self-doubt, unbelief, and rebellion. Delay also opens the door to the opinion of people, which, at best, is only human opinion.

Abraham's life was that of continuous faith and obedience. In Genesis 17:1, God renewed His covenant with Abraham by asking him to circumcise himself and all the men in his house. Even though Abraham was a man in his old age (ninety-nine years old) when he received the command (divine order) to circumcise himself and every man in his household, Abraham did not hesitate. Abraham did not argue rather, he promptly obeyed. The Bible says: "On that very day Abraham took his son Ishmael and every other male in his household and circumcised them, cutting off their foreskins, exactly as God had told him; Abraham was ninety nine years old at that time" (Gen. 17:23–24).

Perhaps of all the dangerous and risky steps of faith that Abraham took in quick response to God's instructions, the story of his willingness to sacrifice his son, Isaac, as a burnt offering to God is one of the greatest acts of prompt obedience in recorded human history. On that fateful day, the Lord called Abraham and told him exactly what to do: "Take your son, your only son—yes, Isaac, whom you love so much—and go to the land of Moriah. Sacrifice him there as a burning offering on one of the mountains, which I will point out to you" (Gen. 22:2). Abraham's response was quick and immediate. Notice that Abraham did not get up after one week or two weeks or perhaps, even after one month, to obey God's voice. Rather, God's Word says: "The next morning, Abraham got up early" (Gen. 22:3). Abraham did not waste time arguing with God or spending endless hours reasoning it out with his wife, Sarah. Apparently, due to his passion for God and the sense of urgency in his heart to obey, Abraham may not have discussed or seek the opinion of his wife on the matter. Rather, Abraham got up, saddled his donkey, split the wood, and took two of his servants along with Isaac, and left (Gen. 12:3).

However, someone may ask: "Why did God ask Abraham to perform human sacrifice? Why was it necessary for God to test Abraham's faith? Why did God ask Abraham to travel about fifty miles from Beersheba to Mt. Moriah (about three days journey) to sacrifice Isaac? We may not be able to provide all the satisfactory answers to these intriguing questions. However, it is important to note that:

> "pagan nations practiced human sacrifice, but God condemned this as a terrible sin (Leviticus 20:1–5). God did not want Isaac to die; He wanted Abraham to sacrifice Isaac in his heart so it would be clear that Abraham loved God more than he loved his promised and long-awaited son. God was testing Abraham. The purpose of testing is to strengthen our character and deepen our commitment to God and his perfect timing. Through "this difficult experience, Abraham strengthened his commitment to obey God. He also learned about God's ability to provide,"

Abraham's prompt and complete obedience found great approval in God's sight. Abraham found favor with God. God renewed His covenant with Abraham to bless and prosper him and his descendants all because of the quickness, completeness, and perfection of Abraham's obedient faith.

> Then the angel of the Lord called again to Abraham from heaven, "This is what the Lord says: Because you have obeyed me and have not withheld your beloved son, I swear by my own self that I will bless you richly. I will multiply your descendants into countless millions, like the stars of the sky and the sand on the seashore. They will conquer their enemies, and through your descendants, all the nations of the earth will be blessed all because you have obey me." (Gen. 22:15–18).

Philip Obeyed Promptly

Another Bible character who demonstrated an exemplary lifestyle of prompt obedience to the marching orders of the Holy Spirit is Philip, the great evangelist whose revival outreach ministry shook the entire gentile city of Samaria. Philip's powerful gospel preaching was confirmed by many miracles of healing and deliverance from witchcraft. The blind could see. The mute could talk. Even the lame could walk. There was great rejoicing, celebration, and jubilation by the people of Samaria as a result of Philip's ministry. Later, the apostles sent Peter and John to witness the awesome demonstration of God's power through Philip. Samaria became the first Gentile town to embrace the gospel. It was in the midst of such a mighty move of God as a result of the prospering ministry of Philip that something totally unexpected happened.

One day, an angel of the Lord suddenly appeared to Philip, instructed him to leave Samaria, and accept the Lord's leading for a new phase of ministry. Philip did not argue. Philip did not question the wisdom of God for such a direction, especially when his ministry was prospering and the young church in Samaria, who were seemingly in desperate need of his attention. How could Philip go to the desert of Gaza for a new assignment when he had become too familiar with an urban ministry? Could such a new lead be from God? Whereas other men and women of God today under similar circumstances as Philip found himself may have been highly tempted to remain in Samaria, perhaps assuming new ecclesiastical titles, Philip refused to perpetrate himself as the new bishop or apostle of Samaria. Rather, Philip promptly, unquestionably, and diligently obeyed the new marching orders of the Holy Spirit. Without question, Philip left and took off for Gaza (a desert), the new place of his divine assignment. The rest is now history. The Holy Spirit has carefully preserved the story of Philip's encounter with the angel in the Bible and Philip's encounter with the Ethiopian eunuch for our inspiration and encouragement.

> As for Philip, an angel of the Lord said to him, "Go South down the desert road that runs from Jerusalem to Gaza." So he did, and helmet the treasurer of Ethiopia, a eunuch of great authority under the queen of Ethiopia. The eunuch had gone to Jerusalem to worship, and he was returning. Seated in his carriage,

he was reading aloud from the book of the prophet Isaiah. The Holy Spirit said to Philip, "Go over and walk along beside the carriage." Philip ran over and heard the man reading from the prophet Isaiah; so he asked, "Do you understand what you are reading?" The man replied, "How can I, when there is no one to instruct me?" and he begged Philip to come up into the carriage and sit with him. The passage of scripture had been reading was this: "He was led as a sheep to the slaughter. And as a lamb is silent before the shavers; he did not open his mouth. He was humiliated and received no justice. Who can speak of his descendants? For his life was taken from the earth. The eunuch asked Philip, "Was Isaiah talking about himself or someone else?" So Philip began with this same scripture and then used many others to tell him the good News about Jesus. As they rode along, they came to some water, and the eunuch said, "Look! There's some water! Why can't I be baptized?" he ordered the carriage to stop, and they went down into the water, and Philip baptized him. When they came up out of the water, the Spirit of the Lord caught Philip away. The eunuch never saw him again. Meanwhile, Philip found himself farther, North at the city of Azotus! He preached the Good News there and line very city along the way until he came to Caesaria. (Acts 8:26–40)

Principles of Prompt Obedience

If we desire revival and a sustained anointing of the Holy Spirit in our lives, then we need to understand some basic principles (elements) of prompt obedience. God values our prompt and complete obedience more than our personal sacrifices and service in His kingdom. We cannot bribe God with our multiplied religious activities, as long as what He wants still remains undone. Always remember that you cannot manipulate God. You cannot manipulate the Holy Spirit. In God's scheme of things, prompt obedience comes first. In other words, there is nothing you do or say in this life, which can take the place (replace) of prompt and unquestionable obedience to do the will of God whatever "doing the will of God" means in your life. If God has told you what you need to do, do not think that the passage of time will make up for your act of disobedience. As long as you are living in disobedience, every act of service, no matter how beautiful and sacrificial, is a dissipation of your energy. Do not waste your precious energy, time and resources trying hard to please God when you know deep down in your heart that you are still rebelling against His expressed plan and purpose for your life.

> What is more pleasing to the Lord: your burnt offerings and sacrifices or your obedience to his voice? Obedience is far better than sacrifice. Listening to him is much better than offering the fat of rams. Rebellion

> is as bad as the sin of witchcraft, and stubbornness is
> as bad as worshipping idols. (1 Sam. 15:22–24)

Prompt Obedience is Costly

Prompt obedience is tough and risky. It is never easy anywhere in the world to do the will of God. The path obedience is the path of trials, pain, misunderstanding, rejection, and even death. Jesus paid the supreme price by dying a horrible and shameful death on a cross as a direct result of His coming into the world in perfect obedience to the will of the Father. Many Christians make the mistake of thinking that because something is God's will, it will be stress-free. They wonder: why shouldn't those who are doing the will of God be shielded from facing shame and disgrace? They often forget that when God asks His people to carry out His will, He does not reveal the complete picture all at once. And even in instances where God gives a person the total picture at the beginning, He may not reveal the step-by-step process of arriving or reaching the ultimate goal. The Lord wants His people to live by faith and learn to trust Him completely, including all the obstacles and challenges in our journey to destiny right from the beginning. We may become too scared to take the first step; thus, aborting our destiny right from the start.

God is a wise father. He tell us what to do and then guides us step-by-step over a period of time to accomplish His purpose for our lives. In the process, He uses the challenges we face during the journey to develop our character and refine our faith. There is a big difference between *vision* and *method*. Many believers see their vision clearly. They know where they are going; but there's great confusion on their mind regarding the type of method the Holy Spirit chooses to use to bring them to their desired destiny. They fail to understand that sometimes God will *dis*organize you in order to *re*organize you later. God's ways are not our ways and God's thoughts are not our thoughts. Because God always has the total picture, with the entire geographical terrain and landscape before His all-seeing eyes, the paths He chooses to take to bring us to our goal may be completely different from our own very limited knowledge. The call to prompt obedience is a call to die. Doing the will of God and answering God's call to Christian service will set you in direct collision course with earthly systems. For no apparent reason, you will be hated by people; you may even be betrayed by your closest friends, associates, and family members. Be ready for the worst in life because you will be hated. You will be sold. You will be banished. And you will be greatly misunderstood and crucified.

Are you willing to do God's will regardless of the circumstances? Are you willing to die so that God's overriding purpose and plan becomes fulfilled in your lifetime and in the succeeding generations after you?

> Stop loving this evil world and all that it offers you,
> for when you love the world, you show that you do

not have the love of the Father in you. For the world offers only the lust for physical pleasure, the lust for everything we see, and pride in our possessions. These are not from the Father. They are from this evil world. And this world is fading away, along with everything it craves. But if you do the will of God, you will live forever. (1 John 2:15–17)

Our Obedience Must Be Prompt and Complete (total)

It was Pastor Enoch A. Adeboye, general overseer of the Redeemed Christian Church of God (RCCG) in Nigeria, West Africa, who captured in his devotional, *Open Heavens* what it means to obey God fully:

> If you want something supernatural to come out of your ordinary situation, you must learn to obey God without complaints or questions. Questioning divine commands is an act of unbelief capable of derailing your trip to boom. Isaiah 1:19 says that blessings ride on two tyres willingness and obedience. How obedient are you to the Lord's instructions? In addition to obedience, there is need for total or complete obedience. Whenever a detail is ignored in a divine assignment, that obedience is incomplete. Leaders have ways of man-ipulating records and figures to appear when they are not. An example of incomplete obedience is recorded of Kings Saul in 1 Samuel 15:15–23. He was asked to kill all the Amalekites both

humans and animals but he spared the king and choice cattle and that cost him his kingdom. In Colossians 3:5, we are commanded to put to death every work of the flesh capable of bringing God's judgment on us. Unfortunately, like King Saul, we decide to kill some and spare some to our detriment. Some people are justifying or rationalizing their weakness. Some argue that it is impossible for a man to be without any fault or occasional lust. That "little" work of the flesh can rob you of your "kingdom" like King Saul. Never spare any weakness you observe in your life. Immediately deal with it. Cry to God to help you or else, it will deal with you. However, according to 2 Corinthians 10:6, until your obedience is complete God may not deal with certain crucial issues in your life. Is your obedience total? Supply whatever is lacking and let your obedience not be wanting"

If you can fully obey God, you are made for life on earth and in heaven. Prompt obedience brings rich rewards The rewards of prompt obedience are unquestifiable. Prompt obedience is extremely rewarding, both in this life and in eternity. The rich blessings of prompt obedience include: favour, joy, perfect peace, protection, security, freedom from fear, divine connections, divine intervention, fruit-bearing, focus and direction, wisdom, fresh anointing, revelation knowledge, double anointing, etc. Prompt obedience yields eternal dividends. Prompt obedience is all gain, with nothing to lose. Disobedience brings tragic consequences.

In Deuteronomy 28, the Bible lists the great blessings of prompt and complete obedience; but at the same, revealing numerous regrettable consequences (curses) of a rebellious life. King Saul is a perfect example of a man who lived in rebellion and disobedience to the marching orders of the Holy Spirit. As a result, he fell from the pinnacle of success to the pit of shame and disgrace. For about forty years or so, King Saul was running the kingdom of Israel without God. The Holy Spirit departed from him (1 Sam. 16:14).